GW00580073

ACCENT

ELLEN DAVIES

INDEPENDENT INNOVATIVE INTERNATIONAL

Published by Cinnamon Press
Meirion House,
Glan yr afon,
Tanygrisiau
Blaenau Ffestiniog,
Gwynedd, LL41 3SU
www.cinnamonpress.com

The right of Ellen Davies to be identified as author of this work has been asserted by her in accordance with the Copyright, Designs and Patent Act, 1988. Copyright © 2015 Ellen Davies.
ISBN: 978-1-907090-69-0

British Library Cataloguing in Publication Data. A CIP record for this book can be obtained from the British Library.

All rights reserved. No part of this publication may be reproduced, stored in a retrieval system, or transmitted in any form or by any means, electronic, mechanical, photocopying, recording or otherwise without the prior written permission of the publishers. This book may not be lent, hired out, resold or otherwise disposed of by way of trade in any form of binding or cover other than that in which it is published, without the prior consent of the publishers.

Designed and typeset in Palatino by Cinnamon Press.
Cover design by Jan Fortune.
Printed in Poland

Cinnamon Press is represented in the UK by Inpress Ltd and in Wales by the Welsh Books Council

Acknowledgements

'Sewing Lessons' appeared in Popshot Magazine and 'Grave Flowers' in Black Sheep Journal.

Contents

Accent

Making Sandwiches

I only asked if I could make my own sandwich,
as the sight of you manhandling
the meat made me sick. I guess
you don't like to think your hands are unclean
or that I don't want you to prepare lunch,
so you begin to shout,
though that's not what I mean,
and your mistake makes me mad.
I'm sure they're perfectly clean
but I don't want your meaty
fingers fouling my food,
though I don't answer back, instead,
I swallow my anger like bile, choke
the witty replies forming in my throat, shackle
my hands to my sides, until the release
of outdoors, my fist bursts
against the wood of the gate,
tearing my knuckles. I bring my torn hand
to my mouth and taste the sweet relief of blood.

Leftovers

Dishes of leftovers,
lined up in the fridge;
a handful of peas,
a sliver of fat, cut
from Sunday's beef,
a smattering of potatoes,
salvaged from plates.
You arrange the containers,
side by side, carefully covered.
No portion is too small to save.
We can't eat them now,
your collection reserved
for a day when supplies
will be scarce. Only then
can we feast on spoilt food.

Ice Cream Call

Three o clock, and so we wait,
for the mechanic jingle,
the hum of the ice cream van
crawling through terraced streets.
We hear it before it arrives,
the faint melody whispering
from a few rows over.
We hold scavenged 50ps
hot in our hands, the crown
a sweaty imprint on our palms.

And then the pull of the engine,
the call, and we burst into a run,
slamming doors hastily behind us,
sandals pounding the tarmac.

We trade our coins for cones, savouring
the cold vanilla bite, the sweet
strawberry sauce as it begins to drip,
too soon, between sticky fingers.

Cymraeg yw iaith yr ysgol

Strictly a language for school,
I left that strange speech
at the gates, itching to utter aloud
the forbidden words I've been harbouring
between my lips all day, words
I've been careful not to be caught with,
smuggled like sins. We only dared whisper
them amongst ourselves in corridors,
empty classrooms; delicious secrets.

Cymraeg oedd iaith yr ysgol,
and so we traded it in, claiming
English for our own, but I search
for it now and cannot think
of how to say `speechless`,
or how to explain my dumb tongue.

Accent

I'm conscious, suddenly,
of my Valleys' drawl,
the clucking at the base
of my throat, my haitches
that hang, disobedient,
from the start of words.
I can hear the lilt
of my As, my Os
dragging their feet.
I try, and fail, to clip
them short. I'm sure
they're laughing at me now,
at the rapid jumble of letters
escaping from my lips.
I've never felt so Welsh.
I'll never speak again.

Ein cwsg cyntaf

It began tentative, slow,
we slept like soldiers,
the crook of your back brushing mine;
separate slumber.

Seizing our chance,
we nestled in my single bunk
under borrowed blankets
hashed together to shelter two,
uncomfortable, close.

Morning: our crude imprint on clean sheets,
the outline of your shape in dawn shadows,
faint traces of our shared scent
lingering.

Cysgu'n Drwm

Those nights your touch became common,
conclusive, a marriage, sealed,
an unconscious kiss in the darkness.

The solid weight of your warmth,
your hand on my hip, now heavy
with sleep, your hot, shallow breath
on the nape of my neck.

Tonight I feel the coolness of your bedside,
your absence, a death.
I stare at the shock of white
where your head does not lie,
ruffling feathers.

Tacluso'r Gwely

Afterwards, you leave me to tidy up,
to smooth the swollen mass of sheets.
I run my palm along the duvet,
ironing out the frantic hollow
with the flat of my hand.
I pull the covers taut, straighten the corners,
feeling the crisp cotton between my fingers.
The room still smells of us, my perfume,
your sweet tang. The pillow wears the imprint
of your head; I pick it up and shake it,
urging it into shape, and stand back.
It looks the same now, corrected,
repaired; our fit of passion spent.

Speck

I found your hair nestled
in the crook of my knee,
too course and dark to be mine.
I hold it lightly between fingers.
It's been weeks since you last lay
in the folds of my sheets
but I find you still, your hair,
your skin stroking mine,
so I savour the single follicle,
the simple promise, a speck of you.

Chained Promise

I've heard that in Paris people,
lovers, shackle their hopes
to a bridge, threading padlock
through grille, an iron embrace.
The key they throw into the depths
of the Seine to be lost, swallowed
by the dark swell. Those locks,
rows of chained promises.

But we never made it to Paris.
I leave the key by our bedside
for you to find.

Art

I lie posed, poised on the stretched canvas of your bed,
your artist eyes search my shape,
noting the delicate dance of light
and shadow on my dimpling skin.
Your hands hesitate, afraid to draw
 the first faint line,
to mould the soft blur of my flesh
into a graphite fact.

Tentatively, you touch the lip
of your pencil
to the crisp paper,
that first line rips a gash,
a tear into which you transfer the familiar
contours of my form.

With each sharp stroke I feel
the solid mass
of my body
coded,
encrypted,
a cipher for which only you hold the key.

I do not suppose it looks like me now,
the darkened hollow of my hips, over pronounced,
the arching curve of my back, too sensuous.
Your delicate dexterity,
warm fingers on my etched face.
Revealing more than I can see.

Grave Flowers

I stare at the garish yellow
of the bulbs straining
against the green gasp
of their leaves,
aching to stretch their necks
towards the sun,
and think of you,
tightly bound in folds
of crushing coal
fighting to free your limbs
so that you too can reach,
edge,
closer
to the clamouring light.

Coming Home

Churned from the earth, the miners come,
revived together, one by one.
Churned from the earth the miners rise,
deathly black with weary white eyes.

Thirty men dead in an explosion of fire,
the pit head blazed, a funeral pyre.
Thirty men's souls swallowed by the earth,
tonight's full moon will see their rebirth.

The wheel starts turning, drawing them up,
with rusted hinges from the withering gut.
The wheel starts turning, spewing them out,
from earth caverns with their deafening shouts.

The moon's yellow glow calls them to arms,
with promises of light and deliverance from harm.
The moon's yellow glow awakens their souls,
hear the pit klaxon cry its death toll.

With burning lungs and heavy tread,
they begin their descent; march of the dead.
With burning lungs and rotted boots,
they stumble down old Workman's Route.

Listen.

Their boots on the bridges banging a beat,
they trudge towards terraced streets.
Their boots on the bridges; the long walk home,
tired and breathless on their celestial roam.

...

I wait.
Face pressed against the cool glass.
Listening for heavy footsteps,
that steady rhythm, a funeral march,
signalling their slow descent.

He shall be here soon.

I prepare his supper,
the familiar process of folding
the soft bread, creasing it at the corners
so that the fleshy crust
can be removed, clean.
Lashings of butter, jam spread thick.
Tea, a sugar sweetened broth
kept warm so that the kettle's whistle
doesn't mask the sound
of his footfall
approaching home.

Our best tablecloth
reserved for births, marriages,
deaths.
I spread it out on the rough tiles of the doorstep,
newly scrubbed.
The wedding crockery wiped free of its storage dust.

And then you are here,
illuminated by the flicker of streetlamps,
coal-clad,
rusted.

I know you cannot come in,
nor eat the meal I offer you,
but stand staring,
with those hollow white eyes,
poised on the porch
you can no longer cross,
still hoping for home.

Soon it will be done,
the first blink of daylight will draw
you back to that dark den.

Returned to the earth, that restless soul,
consigned to his grim grave, buried in coal.

Black and Blue

My uncle has a small blue scar on his left cheek. As a child I thought he'd had an accident with a biro, had drawn a tentative tick on his skin, smudging the ink into his pores with absent minded fingers. He tells me now that it's not ink, but coal, that crept into his cut, dying it navy. I think of the fine black dust nestled beneath his pink surface and shudder. I wonder whether he bleeds blue.

After the funeral

After the funeral you had to learn
to shop for yourself,
to ignore cashiers' sorry smiles.
Meals for one, microwaved,
Nan never trusted you with the oven
after that time you tried to cook a pie
whole, complete with wrapping,
and watched in horror as the box burst
into fierce flames, engulfed in hungry heat.
All that was left was ash.

Loose Tongues

Treachery began
when we were still young,
first careless word whispered,
the shock, sweet taste,
forbidden language
on thirsty tongues- intoxicating.

We lapped it up,
lush linguistic soup,
drinking English dregs,
eating foreign words
whole until they swelled,
swallowed our native speech.

Our betrayal
a noose, strangling the breath
of language. Dead.

Grandcha's Pickles

For as long as I can remember
you've made pickles at Christmas,
great jars of onions peeled and preserved
by your careful hands. As a child
they disgusted me, bulging eyes
bobbing in brown vinegar,
I couldn't see the appeal
until I dared a bite,
a shy nibble and discovered
the sour tang, the crunch of layers
beneath my teeth, the dripping juice,
the kick at the back of my throat
and loved it.

So your pickles were shared amongst family
and we revelled in their secret flavour,
but last year, we had to settle for shop bought,
strange silverskins, brassy white.
Two rounds of chemo meant you couldn't
feel your hands and no one wanted to risk
a pickled finger, but the substitutes were foreign,
disappointing, and the table looked bare
without your second hand jars.

This year you've made pickles again,
you've skinned and soaked them as always
but as I feel the familiar crunch
and taste the bitter homely tang I wonder
if this bite will be my last.
Treatment starts again in January.

Sewing Lessons

Despite your lessons
I never learnt to sew.
I could never master the fluid
movement required to darn a tear
sealing it tight.
Could never emulate the steady rhythm
of your hands as you thread
the faint stitch through the lip
of the ripped fabric.
Your casual flick of the wrist.
The simple knot you tie with a gentle twist,
a bow formed from loose ends
and dangling cotton wisps.
Even now I bring you clothes.
Garments with gashes of flesh missing,
torn out by careless tumbles.
Blazers with burnished buttons slack
from too much wear.
I know what you will say.
I should learn to sew,
to seal up this gasping gulf,
but I bless my ignorant hands.

Rhubarb Crumble

Rhubarb, freshly cut
on an illicit trip to the garden,
still unsteady on your new hip.
I watch you peel back the sinewy
sheaths with expert fingers,
the flat blade balanced between index
and thumb, revealing the bitter root.
The rhubarb must be picked
before it goes to waste, you say,
carefully peeling the salvaged stalks
which have not yet crumbled to seed.

Cancellation

First, you cancel the milk,
sure that you'll never again need
the full four pints. Next,
you tackle the Sky Sports,
his favourite rugby, cricket, gone.
You cancel the papers,
you never had his patience for reading.
You speak of rehoming the dog.
It comes to a head
when we find you stuffing
his dressing gown into a refuse
sack, a few sorry days after
his death. We tell you then,
you can't cancel our crying,
or the stark silence of his vacant chair.

Reading Rebus

I had to buy his new book myself
this time, after years of borrowing
your second-hand copies. I began
aged twelve, too young
to read Rebus, but the crime
didn't faze me, nor did his gruff
familiar silence.

After a brief retirement,
he returned, resurrected
by Rankin's pen.
As I scan another page,
I long for that same power.

Palm Sunday

Palm Sunday brought snow, the ground
hardened with frost, but still you came,
bringing a promise of Spring with your lilac
coat. You unpack the presents slowly,
a clean cloth, bottled water, steadying
yourself on the marble headstone.
You clean the grime from the gold letters,
silently re-reading the psalm that you chose,
pausing at the gap where the letters stop,
that empty gulf of stone. You arrange flowers,
purple tulips and daffs, bought from a place
where Spring has already sprung.
I can feel the hope in it.

Writing poetry in bed
the ghost of an idea
lying beside me in the sheets

Glossary

Cymraeg yw iaith yr ysgol – Welsh is the language of the school

Cymraeg oedd iaith yr ysgol – Welsh was the language of the school

Ein cwsg cyntaf – our first sleep

Cysgu'n drwm – sleeping heavily

Tacluso'r gwely – tidying the bed